KILLING BUDDHA

BODHI

INDIA · SINGAPORE · MALAYSIA

ACKNOWLEDGEMENTS

To the great void—
where all words collapse.

To that which remains
when all else is burned.

To the silence before thought,
the fire that devours the seeker.

CONTENTS

Kill Your Spirituality Before it Kills You

You have been *deceived.*

Every word you have read,
every master you have followed,
every meditation you have done—
none of it has brought you closer to truth.

In fact, it has taken you further away.

They told you there is a path. **They lied.**

They told you enlightenment
is something to attain. **They lied.**

They told you to seek.
And so, you have spent your life running
in circles, worshipping ghosts.

You have spent years climbing
a ladder that leads nowhere.
You have memorized scriptures
that have turned to dust in your hands.
You have bowed before false gods,
recited empty mantras,
performed rituals that only
sanctified your ignorance.

And still,
you wonder why you are not *free.*

YOUR SPIRITUALITY IS YOUR PRISON.

You believe you are evolving.
You believe you are becoming
something higher, something purer.

But what if I told you that every step you take
on this so-called path is another step into delusion?

Spirituality is the final trap.

You traded material desires for
spiritual ones, but the hunger remains.

You no longer chase money, fame, or power—
you chase enlightenment, wisdom, peace.

You think this makes you superior.
It only makes you more sophisticated
in your suffering.

A man obsessed with gold is blind.

A man obsessed with God is equally blind.

Do you think there is a difference?

A man went to a temple seeking truth.
The master locked him inside and left.

Years passed.

The man finally saw that the temple was empty.

BURN EVERYTHING YOU BELIEVE.

Now, I tell you this:
Everything you believe about spirituality
must be **burned**.

Religion?
A market of fear. Selling salvation to those
who have been convinced they are sick.

Gurus?
Merchants selling cages made of words,
dressed in robes of illusion.

The "Self"?
A trick of the ego to keep itself alive.

You hold onto these things like
a drowning man clings to a stone.
And then you wonder why
you are sinking.

You do not need more teachings.
You do not need another book.
You need to **undo**.

Undo your concepts.

Undo your identity.

Undo the idea that
there is anything to attain.

Because until you have nothing left,
you will not see what has always been.

IF YOU SEE BUDDHA ON THE ROAD,
KILL HIM.

Not because Buddha is your enemy.
But because you have made him an idol.

You have turned wisdom into a concept,
truth into an object.

You have taken the simplest,
most obvious reality and buried it
under a mountain of words,
practices and beliefs.

If Buddha was here,
he would tell you the same.

He would tell you to
throw away his words,
forget his face, and
walk away.

And yet,
instead of walking away,
you bow before statues,
chant his name, and
repeat his teachings
like a parrot reciting poetry
 it does not understand.

You have made Truth
into a story.
A beautiful, poetic, fiction.
An utterly false story.

Now, I tell you this:
If you see Buddha, kill him.

But what if the Buddha is you?

Would you dare to kill yourself?

Not the body.

Not the mind.

But
the **you**
that believes.
The **you**
that seeks.
The **you** that
wants to be enlightened.

That is the only real death.
That is the only real liberation.

And if you are not
ready for that—
if you still want to hold onto
your scriptures, your practices,
your sacred illusions—
then **close this book.**

It is not for you.

It will burn everything you hold dear.

It will leave you with nothing.

And only then—only then—
will you see what was always there.

CHAPTER 1

The Lie of
the Path

There is no path.
Seeking assumes distance.
Seeking assumes time.

Truth is **neither.**

A path means direction.
A path means progress.
A path means you are moving
from somewhere to somewhere.

But Truth is not a place.

It is not waiting for you
at the end of a road like a
prize for your effort.

Truth
is here.

Now.

Always.

The moment you say,
"I am searching,"
you have already lost.

THE SEEKER IS THE LOST ONE.

You believe you are
on a journey.
You believe you are
accumulating wisdom,
moving closer,
step by step,
like a man climbing
a mountain.

But have you ever seen a mountain climb itself?

A wave can travel the ocean,
but it never leaves the water.

A fish can swim across the sea,
but it was never separate from it.

Yet you, the great spiritual seeker,
believe you are moving towards something
outside yourself.

Who is moving?

A man ran for years
searching for his shadow.
One day, he stopped.
The shadow was never running.

If you truly see this,
the search ends **instantly.**

But if you do not,
you will keep running—
perhaps even reading the next chapter,
thinking there is something more.

THE PATH IS A PRISON.

What if I told you
that the very idea of *"the spiritual path"*
is keeping you trapped?

When you believe you are on a path,
you divide reality.
You create a **before** and an **after**.
You create the illusion of progress.
But in doing so, you also create
the one who is progressing.

And here is the trick:
The one who is progressing does not exist.

This is why all seeking fails.
You are trying to perfect a mirage.
You are attempting to polish an illusion.

When will you see?

A monk asked the master,
"How do I reach the other shore?"

The master replied,
"Who says you are on this one?"

You never left.
There was nowhere to go.

THE LAST STEP IS THE FIRST FALL.

If you believe there is a final step,
you are already lost.
If you believe enlightenment
is waiting at the top of the mountain,
you have already fallen to the bottom.

There are no steps.

There is no mountain.

A monkey in a cage dreams of freedom.

He rattles the bars,
reaches through them,
searches for the key.

But the walls of the cage were never real.
He was free the whole time.

And so I ask you:

What happens if you stop running?

What happens if you let go of the search?

What happens if you stop pretending
there is a "you" who must reach something?

What happens?

Nothing.

And in that nothing,
everything is revealed.

Why You Must Kill Buddha

The Buddha you worship
is your **prison**.

The Buddha you follow
is your **distraction**.

The very moment you bow,
you have lost him.

You believe Buddha is a man.
You believe he was enlightened.
You believe if you follow
his words,
his path,
his discipline,
you will reach
where he did.

Lies.

Buddha was not a man.
Buddha is not a story.
Buddha is not something to be followed.

If you think
you can follow Buddha,
you have already misunderstood
everything.

BUDDHA NEVER WANTED
FOLLOWERS.

People chase spiritual figures
like children chase fireflies.

You read his words.
You build statues.
You chant his name.
And you think this brings you closer?

If you had truly understood Buddha,
you would not be bowing.
You would not be worshipping.
You would not even be here.

*A man searching for Buddha
walked across a desert for seven years.
Finally, he reached a temple where
an old master sat in silence.*

*The man asked,
"Where is the way to Buddha?"*

*The master replied,
"Who is asking?"*

The man disappeared.

Do you understand?

If the one searching is an illusion,
who is there to find anything?

Buddha was only ever pointing at the void.
But you, like all fools, have fallen in love
with the finger.

YOU WANT A MASTER
BECAUSE YOU ARE A COWARD.

Why do you seek a master?
Why do you want a teacher?

Because you are *afraid*.

Afraid to stand alone.
Afraid to look at reality
without a guide,
without a map,
without someone to tell you
what is true.
And so, you run
to the feet of a guru,
a saint, a prophet.

You call them *enlightened*.
You call them *divine*.
You surrender, thinking this will
bring freedom.

But your surrender is slavery.
Your devotion is fear.
Your master is a crutch.

Buddha would have spat on your obedience.

A real master is not here to comfort you.
A real master will shake you, mock you,
throw you into the abyss, and watch you drown.
If your master is kind, if he gives you hope,
if he makes you feel safe—he is your enemy.

*A disciple asked,
"What is the way to enlightenment?"*

The master kicked him in the chest.

*The disciple fell to the ground,
gasping for air.*

*The master said,
"That."*

KILL THE BUDDHA IN YOUR MIND.

Buddha is **not** a man.
Buddha is **not** a religion.
Buddha is **not** an idea.
Buddha is what remains
when you are **gone**.

But instead of vanishing,
you have made him an idol.

You have placed him
in temples,
in books,
in your prayers.
You have locked him
inside your mind and
called it wisdom.

Now, I tell you this:
If you want truth,
you must kill every Buddha you find
especially the one in your mind.

If you see Buddha,
burn his words.

If you see Buddha,
shatter his statues.

If you see Buddha,
walk away.

Because the real Buddha
is not something you can see.
Not something you can know.
Not something you can hold onto.

And until you have killed him,
you will never be free.

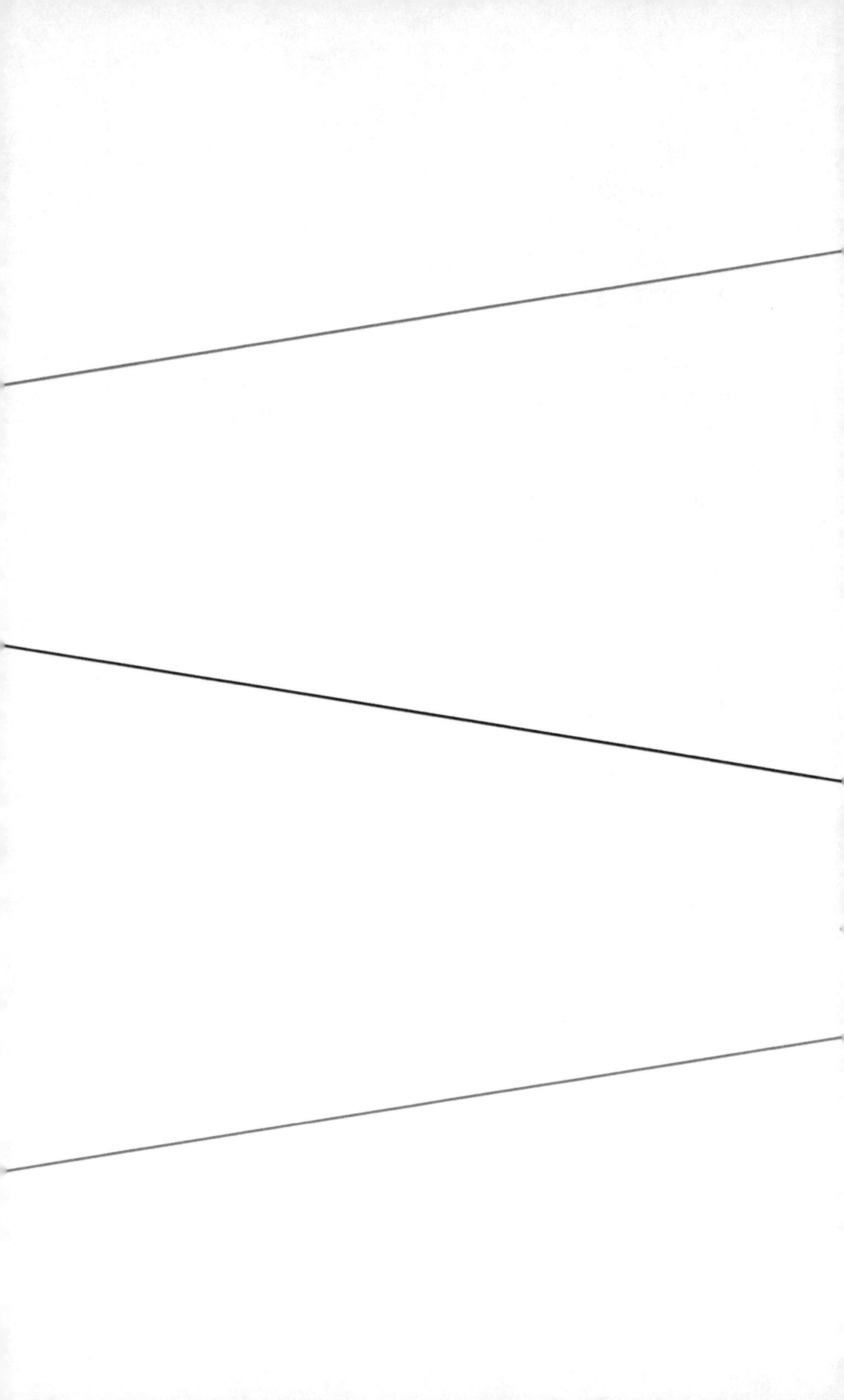

CHAPTER 3

Leaning Tower of Buddha

You build gods like you build towers—
higher and higher, hoping to reach the sky.
But the taller the statue,
the farther you are from its essence.

You carve divinity from stone,
place it on a pedestal, and kneel before it.
You build temples, churches, mosques—
monuments to your own blindness.

You chant its name,
light your candles,
bow your head.
And with every act of worship,
you bury the truth a little deeper.

A monkey saw a coconut tree and
thought the fruit was closer to the stars.
He climbed higher,
reached for the sky,
and fell.

You are that monkey.

Reaching.
Climbing.
Convinced that if you
just build a god high enough,
just pray hard enough,
just believe deeply enough—
you will touch something real.

WHEN EGO WEARS A HALO.

But worship is never about God.
It is about *you*.

You don't kneel in devotion.
You kneel in ownership.
"This is my God. My truth. My path."
The ego wraps itself in devotion
like a wolf in monk's robes.

And now,
instead of *power*,
it seeks *purity*.
Instead of *wealth*,
it seeks *virtue*.
But it is still seeking.
Still grasping.

A man once built a temple and
prayed to be free from his ego.
One day, he left the temple.

But before he stepped outside,
he turned back, looked at it, and smiled.
"What a beautiful temple I built," he said.

The ego does not disappear.
It just changes clothes.

THE PRISON OF IDEAS.

Once you have built a god,
you must defend it.
The walls must be high.
The gates must be guarded.
No doubt must enter,
no question must be asked.

This is how devotion becomes a cage.
You start by seeking truth, and
you end up fighting to protect a lie.
You start by searching for freedom, and
you end up enforcing rules.

A man found a bird trapped in a cage.
He wanted to set it free. But first,
he painted the cage gold.

This is what you do with your ideas.
You polish them.
Worship them.
Protect them.
Until the bird inside—
the living truth—is *forgotten*.

THE IRONY OF GIANT GODS.

And now, you have made your gods
bigger than ever.

100 feet.
112 feet.
A thousand tons of concrete and steel
reaching for the heavens.
Spiritual centres are busy making
world record bust statues of their gods.
They have become obsessed with size.
Devotion is *measured in feet.*

You stand before them in awe.
You take pictures.
You write about how magnificent they are.
And you miss the *irony* completely.

The Buddha sat beneath a tree with nothing.
You built a 500-foot Buddha and
charge an entry fee.

Christ walked barefoot.
You erected a Jesus so tall it needs an elevator.

Shiva roamed the mountains.
You trapped him in blackened steel
sheet metals and floodlights.

What are you really worshipping?

Not truth.
Not divinity.

Just your own construction.

*A man spent his life
building a bridge to heaven.
When he reached the end, he realized—
there was nowhere to go.*

LET THE TOWER COLLAPSE.

The gods you build are not for worship.
They are for hiding behind.

If your god is so great,
why do you need a statue?
If your truth is so real,
why do you need a temple?

You do not need gods
made of stone.
You do not need towers
that reach the sky.

*A man once spent his life
carving a perfect idol of God.
When he finally finished, he stood back,
admired his work, and wept.*

Not because he had found God—
but because he had lost himself.

Let the tower **collapse.**
See what remains.

CHAPTER 4

The Uselessness of Meditation

Sitting in silence
will not awaken you.

Staring at a wall
will not dissolve the illusion.

Counting your breath
will not free you from yourself.

Meditation, as a technique,
becomes another illusion.

You think meditation will
purify you.
You think it will make you
empty,
enlightened,
whole.

But the one meditating
is the one who keeps you trapped.

The mind that **meditates**
is the mind that **dreams.**

The mind that **sits**
is the mind that **clings.**

The mind that **watches**
is the mind that **divides.**

Do you not see?
Meditation is another game.

THE MIND THAT MEDITATES
IS THE MIND THAT SUFFERS.

People meditate thinking
they will achieve something.

They call it **mindfulness**.
They call it **presence**.
They call it **transcendence**.

But all they are doing
is chasing.

You say,
"I am meditating."
The moment you say this,
you have already
fallen into the trap.

Who is meditating?
Who is watching the breath?
Who is controlling thought?

It is the same self
that **suffers**.
The same self
that **craves**.
The same self
that **pretends** to be free.

A man sits cross-legged,
eyes closed, chasing stillness.

A dog chases its own tail,
convinced freedom is just a turn away.

What is the difference?

*A man sat in perfect stillness
for ten years.
One day, a bird shat on his head.
He realized he had wasted a decade.*

STILLNESS IS NOT WHAT YOU THINK.

But this does not mean
stillness is useless.
True stillness is not
the absence of movement;
it is the absence of resistance.

Stillness is **not** controlling breath.
Stillness is **not** forcing silence upon yourself.
Stillness is **not**
a discipline,
a practice,
a method.
Stillness happens when there is no two.

No watcher, no watched.
No seeker, no sought.
No meditator, no meditation.

The bird never left stillness.
The tree never left stillness.

But the man—
he was chasing silence
like a beggar chases coins.

WHEN WILL YOU STOP?

Stop.

Right now.
Not gradually.
Not tomorrow.

Now.

Do not close your eyes.

Do not sit like a stone.

Do not try to be still.

Just stop.

Stop seeking.
Stop resisting.
Stop playing the game.

And in that stopping, **see**.

See that stillness is what remains
when you are not.

Not because you achieved it.
Not because you practiced it.
But because it was never missing.

But you—
you were too busy meditating
to notice.

CHAPTER 5

The Ego's Final Trick

The moment you think you have
transcended the ego, it has grown stronger.
The moment you declare yourself free,
you are more bound than ever.

This is the *final trick.*
The **last deception.**

You say,
"I am enlightened."
Who is this I?

You say, "I have no ego."
Who just spoke?

You believe you have escaped,
but you are still in the cage.
You have only painted the bars gold.

THE SHADOW THAT LAUGHS AT YOU.

The ego is like a shadow.
The more you chase it,
the more it moves.
The more you fight it,
the stronger it becomes.

The moment you say,
"I am beyond the self,"
you have only built a new self—
a holier, more refined,
more insidious self.

The spiritual ego is the **most dangerous**.

It does not crave wealth.
It does not crave pleasure.

It craves *awakening*.

And so, the seeker becomes proud
of his humility.
The disciple becomes arrogant
in his surrender.
The wise man becomes blind
in his wisdom.

THE MOUNTAIN OF SELF-DECEPTION.

*A man climbed the tallest mountain
to escape himself.
At the peak,
he found himself waiting.*

You think you are running from the ego,
but you are running in circles.
Every step you take to rid yourself of you—
is taken by you.

Who is renouncing?
Who is purifying?
Who is seeking?
Who is awakening?

Everywhere you go,
you will meet yourself.
Every mask you remove
will reveal another face.

STOP PLAYING THE GAME.

There is only one way out.

Stop.

Do not renounce the ego.
Do not fight the ego.
Do not transcend the ego.

Simply *see* it.

See it for what it is—
just movement,
just thought,
just wind passing through
an empty room.

And in that moment of seeing—
effortless, untouched—it is gone.
Not because you killed it.
Not because you mastered it.

But because
it was never there.

CHAPTER 6

The Cult of Spirituality

Spirituality is just
another marketplace.
And you are
the perfect customer.
You think you are seeking truth.
But you are just shopping.

ENLIGHTENMENT FOR SALE.

Gurus sell wisdom
like merchants sell junk.
They wrap emptiness in gold.
They whisper sweet nothings
and call it liberation.

Bookshelves overflow
with enlightenment—
for a hefty price.

Meditation apps
promise inner peace
in five minutes a day.

Retreats offer salvation,
all-inclusive, starting at
INR 50,000.

And you buy it all.

You spend your life collecting
spiritual words,
spiritual techniques,
spiritual identities.

You weigh your worth in
the number of books you've read,
the number of retreats you've attended,
the number of spiritual phrases you can recite.

You left one cult only to join another.

THE GOD THAT SELLS YOU
BACK TO YOURSELF.

*A man entered a temple
and saw God.*

He left immediately.

*Why?
Because he saw the scam.*

He saw the god who only existed
as long as people worshipped.
He saw the temple built not for truth,
but for followers.
He saw the *business of belief.*

Every religion is a corporation.
Every guru is a salesman.
Every teaching is a product.

And yet,
you kneel.

THE ONLY WAY OUT.

There is only one way
to escape the cult.

Stop believing.

Do not believe in gods.
Do not believe in masters.
Do not believe in teachings.

And most of all—
do not believe in yourself.

Because the greatest cult
is the one inside your head.

The cult of I.

And until you break free from that,
you will keep buying illusions.

CHAPTER 7

No One Wakes Up

You think awakening
happens to a person.
But there is no person.

You think enlightenment
is something you attain.
But there is no you.

This is why all seeking fails.
**Because the one seeking
does not exist.**

THE DREAM THAT DREAMS ITSELF.

A wave cannot wake up
from the ocean.
It can rise, it can fall—
but it never left the water.

You cannot wake up
from the dream because
you are the dream.

Everything you take yourself to be—
your name,
your past,
your thoughts,
your beliefs—
is just movement on the surface.

But does the ocean ever move?
Yes.

Does it ever leave itself?
No.

THIS IS STILLNESS.

Stillness is not something you do.

Stillness is when nothing is separate.

Not the ocean and the wave.
Not the dancer and the dance.
Not the seeker and the sought.

You say,
"I am meditating,
I am surrendering,
I am dissolving."

But **who** is meditating?
Who is surrendering?
Who is dissolving?

There is **no one** there.

Only the mind pretending to disappear,
while secretly hoping to remain.

THE FINAL QUESTION.

A student asked,
"Master, when will I wake up?"

The master said,
"Who is sleeping?"

The student was silent.

Not because he understood.
But because he was no longer there to ask.

And that silence—
effortless,
thoughtless,
without a center—
was the answer.

CHAPTER 8

The Spiritual Addict

You are not spiritual.

You are addicted to
the idea of being spiritual.

You hoard techniques like
a monkey hoards stolen fruit—
grasping,
clutching,
piling them up,
afraid to let go.

Every retreat,
every mantra,
every fast,
every ritual—

A desperate attempt
to convince yourself
you are getting
somewhere.

But you are not
getting *anywhere.*
You are running in a circle and
calling it a path.

THE FIX THAT NEVER SATISFIES.

You **chase** silence.
You **chase** bliss.
You **chase** something called
"awakening."

You tell yourself
it's about truth,
**but truth does not
need to be chased.**

What you really want
is a high that never ends.

You are no different from
the drunkard clutching his bottle,
except your poison comes wrapped
in incense and chanting.

That's why you keep searching.

That's why you keep consuming.

**The moment one technique stops working,
you replace it with another.**

One day it's Vipassana.
Next, it's psychedelics.
Next, it's tantra.
Next, it's Advaita.

Yesterday,
you were **dissolving** the ego.
Today,
you are **manifesting** your desires.

Yesterday,
you were **renouncing** the world.
Today,
you are **aligning** your chakras.

You keep changing the drug,
but the **addiction** stays the same.

The spiritual market knows this.

That's why it never runs out of
new techniques,
new teachers,
new experiences.

A buffet of enlightenment,
endlessly refilled, so you never
leave the table.

But tell me—
has it worked?

EFFORTLESS TRUTH.

The truth does not come
through effort.

It does not come
through struggle.

It does not come
through discipline.

A man tried to
push the river forward.
It kept flowing
without him.

You fight.
You meditate harder.
You breathe deeper.
You force yourself
to sit still,
to chant louder,
to believe stronger.

But truth does not need you.
Reality does not need your effort.

The sun does not rise
because you pray.

The wind does not blow
because you surrender.

The sky does not open
because you have reached
the final level.

Let go of effort.
Let go of letting go.

See what remains.

CHAPTER 9

Letting Go is a Lie

People say, "Just let go."

But who is letting go?

The one who holds
is still there.

The one who holds on
is the same as the one
trying to let go.

Trying to let go
is still holding.

You think surrender is
a choice you can make.
But the truth is,
surrender is the end of choice.

You don't choose to surrender.
You surrender when there is no longer
a **you** to choose.

THE ILLUSION OF CONTROL.

Control is the lie
that keeps you imprisoned.

Trying to control
your thoughts,
your emotions,
your actions—this is all just a **game.**

You are not the controller.
You are not the actor.
You are the stage, the actor,
and the audience—*simultaneously*.

Trying to control
is a trick of the mind,
a false sense of power.

Letting go of control
is not about releasing it;
it's about realizing that
control was never yours
to begin with.

THE TRUTH OF NON-RESISTANCE.

A hand opened to drop the stone.
The stone was never held.

What does it mean
to "let go"?

To drop the stone?

No. The stone was never held.

You never held anything.
The moment you think
you are holding something,

you have already forgotten
that you are the hand,
not the stone.

Stop trying to drop the stone.
See that it was never in your grasp.

Letting go is not something you do.
It is the realization that
nothing has ever been held.
Not your thoughts,
not your fears,
not your past.

Nothing.

THE END OF EFFORT.

The truth cannot be controlled,
nor can it be let go of.

It just is.
When you stop trying to hold,
you will see that nothing was ever held.

And in that moment,
you will realize that
you are the hand,
not the stone.

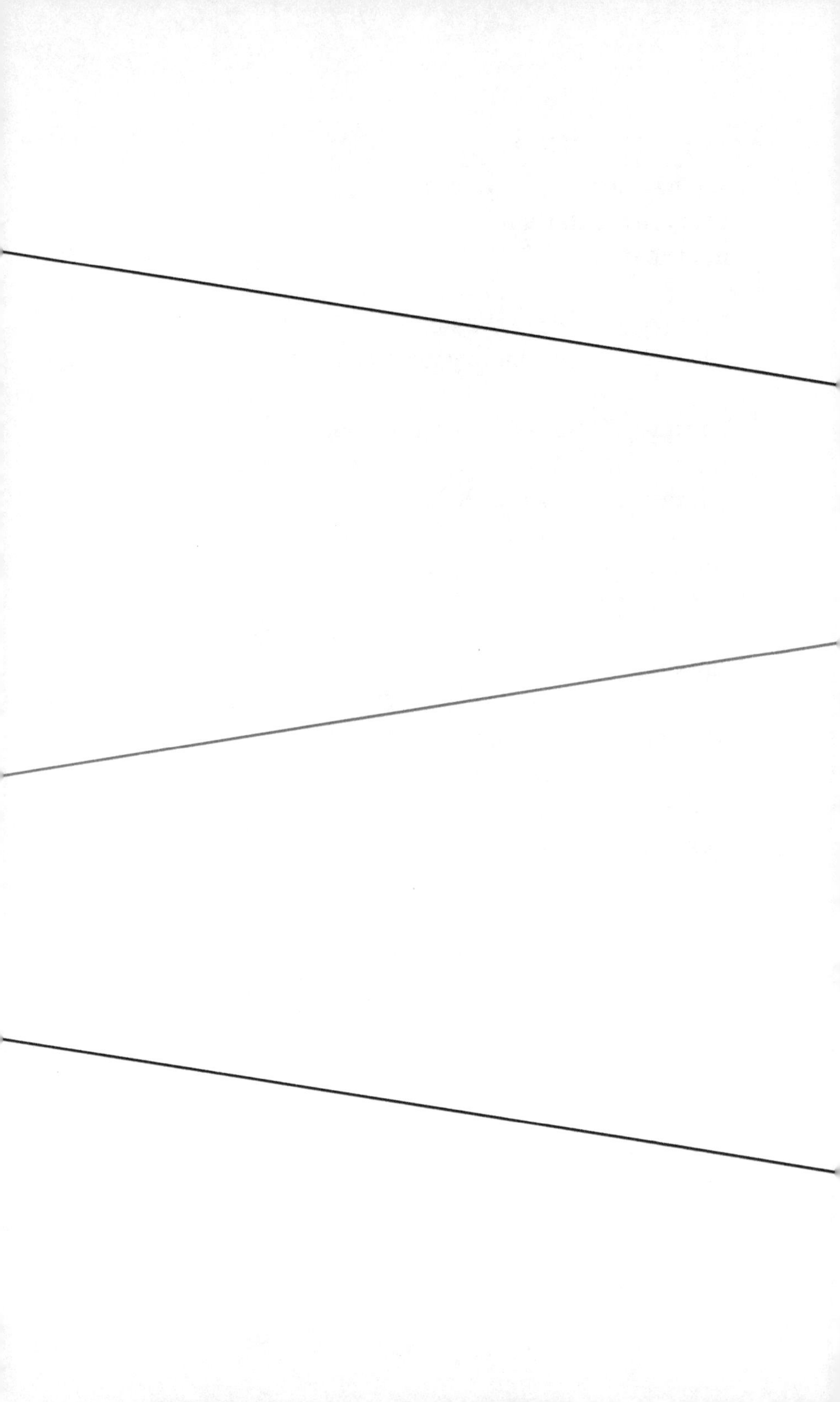

Destroying the Master

The master is a bridge.
Cross it, and leave it behind.

The master is a fire.
Burn in it, and step out as ash.

If your master
still exists in your mind,
you have not yet walked.

If you still bow,
you are still blind.

THE PRISON OF DISCIPLESHIP.

You come to the master
begging for wisdom.
You ask, you listen, you follow.
You surrender at his feet,
thinking surrender
is freedom.

But a disciple is just a shadow.
A reflection of the master, not the sun.

You do not become **wise**.
You become **obedient**.
You do not become **free**.
You become **dependent**.

And as long as you are a disciple,
you will never **see**.

The world is full of devoted followers,
yet empty of awakened beings.

Why?

Because discipleship
is the most beautiful prison.
The walls are built of devotion,
the chains forged from reverence.

And you—
grateful for your cage—
polish the bars and
call it liberation.

THE FINAL LESSON.

A real master exists
only to destroy himself in you.
To make himself unnecessary.

The moment you understand,
he is dead.
And if he is still alive,
you are still sleeping.

A disciple once said,
"Thank you for teaching me."
The master laughed,
"Who taught whom?"

Was the master ever there?
Or was he just a reflection
of your own awakening?

KILL THE MASTER, BURN THE ASHES.

The false master
makes you dependent.
The real master
makes himself disappear.

If you **still** seek his approval,
if you **still** cling to his words,
if you **still** think he holds something
you do not—*you have missed the point.*

A real master does not give you truth.
He takes away your lies.

And when there are no lies left,
what need is there for a master?

The river does not worship the bridge
once it reaches the ocean.

The fire does not remember the match
once it has become ash.

The master is a fire.
Let it burn.

Step out *alone.*

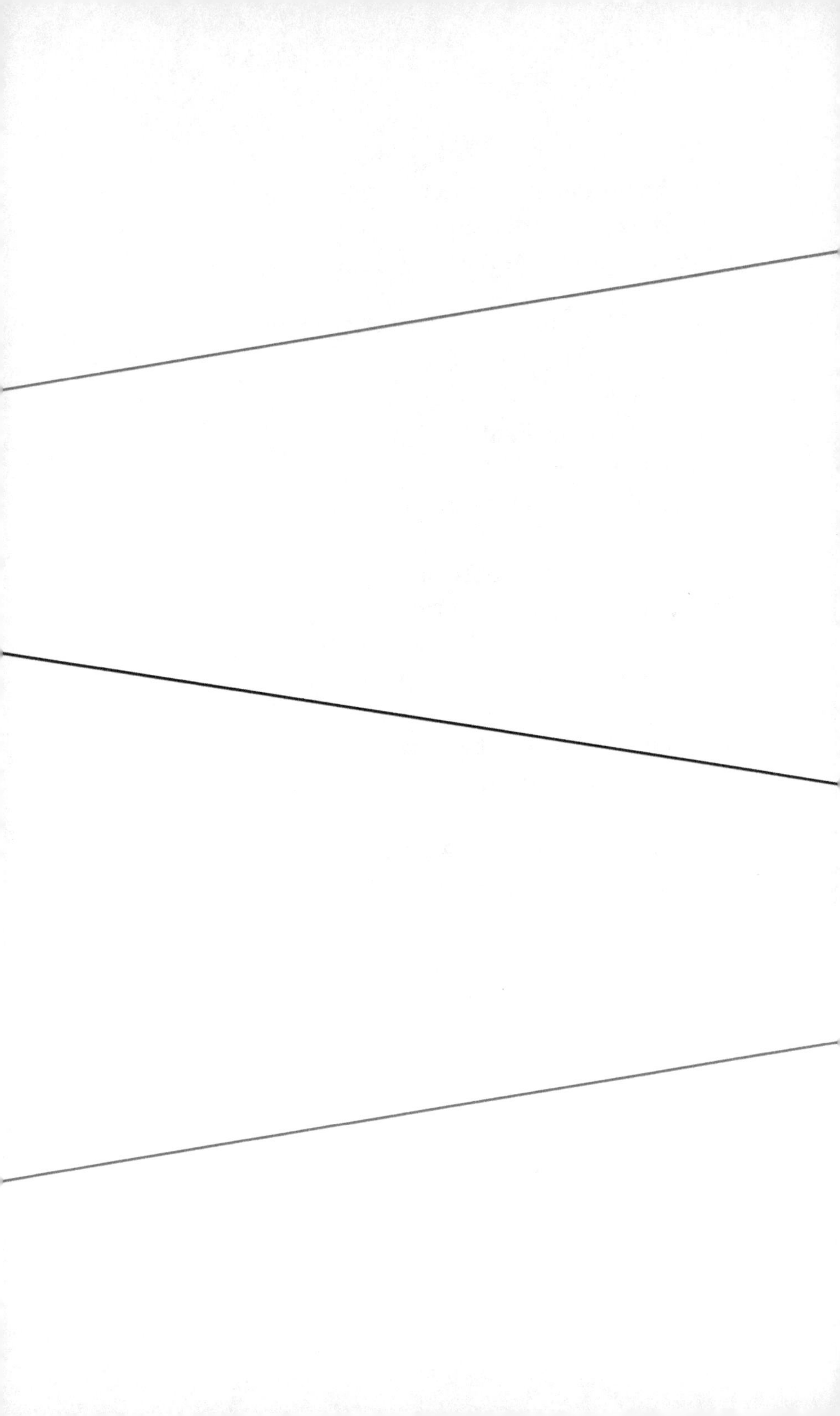

CHAPTER 11

The Myth of Enlightenment

You have been fooled.
You believe enlightenment
is something to attain—
A **reward**,
a **destination**,
a **final moment**
where the heavens part
and truth is revealed.

This is the **greatest lie**.

ENLIGHTENMENT IS NOT GAINED.

You think you must
climb higher,
go deeper,
meditate longer.

You think you must
accumulate wisdom,
purify yourself,
transcend the world.

But enlightenment
is not something added to you.

It is what remains
when everything falls away.
It is not an **achievement**.
It is a **disappearance**.

THE TRUTH OF LOSS.

**The man
who sought everything
lost himself.**

**The man
who lost everything
found himself.**

You don't become enlightened.
You vanish.

The mind that
seeks enlightenment
is the very thing
that obscures it.
The self that
longs for truth
is the very thing
that must dissolve.

Do you understand?

The moment you think,
"I am enlightened,"
there is still an I left
to claim it.

And so,
you are still **blind**.

THE END OF THE SEEKER.

The seeker
and the sought
were never two.

There was no journey.
No path.
No end.

Enlightenment
is simply the absence
of you.

When you stop
trying to hold on,
when there is
nothing left to seek,
nothing left to lose,
nothing left to become—

Only then will you see
what has always been.

CHAPTER 12

Truth Cannot Be Known

The moment you say,
"I know,"
you are **blind**.

The moment you say,
"I understand,"
you are **lost**.

Truth does not belong to you.
It is not something you can own,
not something you can hold.

The more you try to grasp it,
the more it slips through your fingers.

THE PRISON OF KNOWLEDGE.

You think knowledge
will bring you closer.
You read scriptures,
memorize teachings,
follow philosophies.

You collect wisdom
like a donkey carrying books—
loaded with knowledge
not understanding anything.

You hope that enough of them
will buy you freedom.

But truth cannot be bought.

Truth cannot be stored.

Truth cannot be held in the mind.

**A man bottled the ocean.
He opened it and found nothing.**

All your words,
all your ideas,
all your theories—
they are bottles filled with air,
labels stuck to emptiness.

Truth was never inside them.

THE MIND CAN NEVER TOUCH IT.

The mind wants to know
because it is terrified of not knowing.
It builds concepts, beliefs, certainties—
anything to avoid the abyss.

But truth is the abyss.

Truth is what remains
when there is nothing left
to hold on to.

Do you have the courage
to let go?

To stand in the unknown
without grabbing for answers?

THE END OF UNDERSTANDING.

To truly see,
you must stop trying to see.
To truly understand,
you must give up all understanding.

The wind does not
need to be caught.
The ocean does not
need to be bottled.

**Truth does not
need to be known.**

It only needs to *be*.

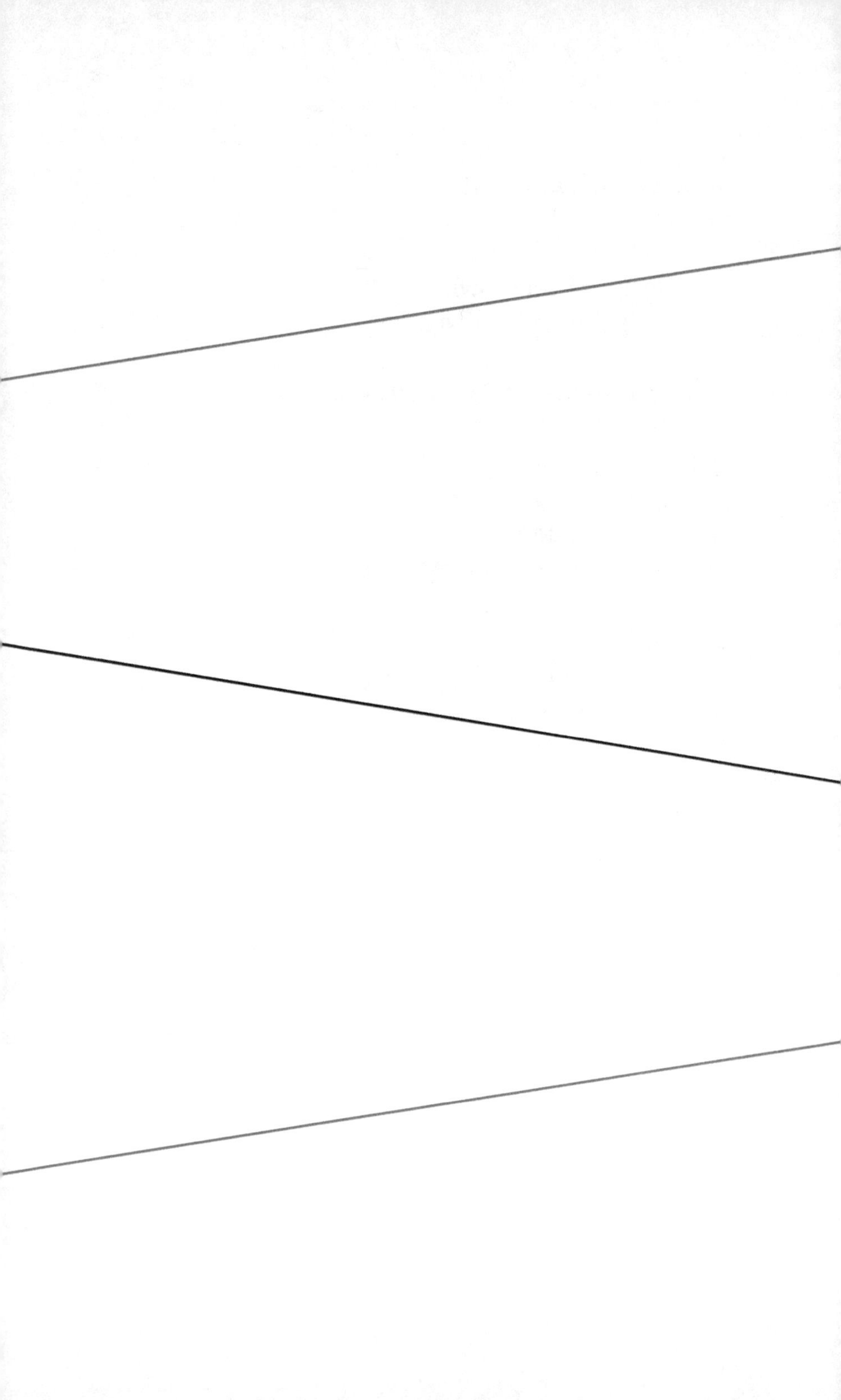

You Were Never Born

You believe you were born.
You believe you have
a past,
a name,
a story.
You believe you are someone
moving through time, heading toward
some inevitable end.

But this is the greatest illusion of all.

**THE BODY WAS BORN—
BUT YOU?**

Yes, the body was born.
Yes, the body will die.

But you—
what are you?
A **collection** of memories?
A **string** of thoughts?
A **name** someone gave you?

Everything you call "yourself"
is borrowed.
Given to you by others,
stitched together by time.

A man searched for his birthplace.
He found it was never built.

Where were you
before birth?
Where will you be
after death?

If you look deeply,
you will see—
you were never here.

THE DREAM OF EXISTENCE.

You are like a wave that believes
it has a separate life from the ocean.
But was the wave ever really born?

Did it ever truly begin?
Or was it always just the ocean, moving?

You, too, are not
what you think you are.
Not a **body**.
Not a **person**.
Not a **separate thing**
floating in time.

You are the ocean.
And the ocean has
no birth,
no death.

SEEING THROUGH THE ILLUSION.

What happens when you
stop believing you were ever born?

What happens when you
stop believing you are moving toward an end?

There is **no beginning**.

There is **no end**.

There is **only this**.

CHAPTER 14

Spit on the Altar

You bow before
gods made of stone.

You whisper prayers
to the sky.

But tell me—
has the sky ever answered?
Has the statue ever spoken?
Has a single prayer ever bent
the laws of existence?

No.

But you keep kneeling.
Because it is easier to beg
than to stand.

**Religion is
the longest-running scam
in history.**

A **business** that sells fear.
A **market** where you trade your life
for an afterlife that does not exist.

They tell you that suffering now
will buy you peace later.
They tell you to bow lower,
to obey,
to accept.

And so,
you spend your days
fasting for a god who is already full,
confessing sins that were never yours,
and kissing the feet of men
who pretend to be holy.

You have never met your god,
yet you live in his shadow.

You have never touched heaven,
yet you waste your life chasing it.
And for what?

*"A man prayed every day for salvation.
One day, he opened his eyes
and saw he was still kneeling."*

How long will you kneel?
How long will you wait for a whisper
that will never come?

Get up.

Walk away.

The altar is empty.
The gods you worship are dead,
and the ones still alive
are laughing at you.

You have built temples for ghosts.
You have poured your devotion
into an empty sky.
And you wonder why
you still feel hollow.

Spit on the altar.

Burn the scripture.

Break the statue.

Then,
see what remains.

CHAPTER 15

The Great Spiritual Conspiracy

The world does not
want you *free*.

A man who wakes up
is useless to society.
He cannot be controlled,
cannot be frightened,
cannot be sold his own salvation.

If you wake up,
who will need their temples?

If you wake up,
who will fear their gods?

If you wake up,
who will buy their enlightenment,
neatly packaged and overpriced?

So they keep you seeking.
They keep you hungry.
They keep dangling enlightenment
like a carrot in front of a blind donkey.

Chase it.
Chase it.
Chase it.

The gurus tell you,
"Just a little more effort."

The scriptures tell you, "
Just a little more discipline."

The world tells you,
"You are not there yet."

And you believe them.

Why?

Because not chasing would mean
facing the terrifying possibility that
there was never anything to chase.
That the whole thing was a trick.
That the finish line was painted
on the ground beneath you.

*"A monkey saw the moon
reflected in a well.
He reached for it
and fell in."*

This is you.

Reaching.
Falling.
Never stopping.

But what happens
when you stop?

The carrot vanishes.

The well disappears.

The monkey sees
the moon was always
in the sky.

Everything they have told you
will **collapse**.

Every structure you believed in
will **burn**.

Every illusion
will **shatter**.

And then—
you will laugh.

Because the greatest joke of all?

You were *never* trapped.

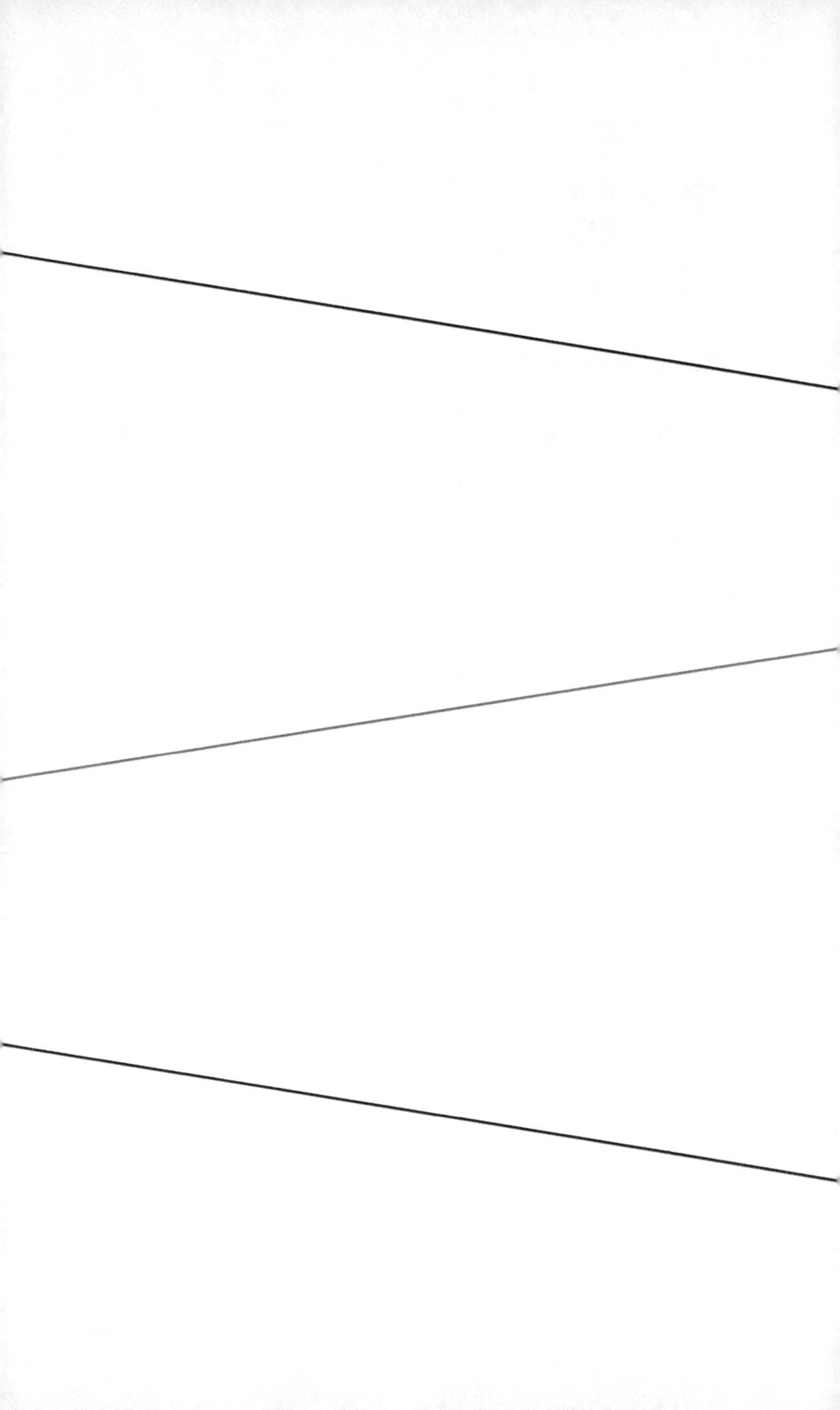

CHAPTER 16

The Final Letting Go

This is
the **last** page.

The **last** teaching.

The **last** illusion to burn.

There is **nothing** after this.

No next step.
No secret waiting to be revealed.

If you are still looking for something,
you have already lost.

You thought this path
would lead somewhere.
That all the seeking,
the meditating,
the breaking,
the surrendering—
would take you to some
great conclusion.

But there is no conclusion.

There is no grand revelation
waiting at the end.

No enlightenment
descending like a thunderbolt.

The final truth
is not a truth at all.
It is the absence of
every truth you have ever
believed in.

NOTHING TO HOLD,
NOTHING TO DROP.

People talk about *surrender*.
People talk about *freedom*.
People talk about *letting go*.

But who is letting go?
Who is there to be free?

You are still searching,
still grasping at some final key
to unlock the door.

But what if there is no door?
What if there never was?

You came here
looking for answers.
Looking for something
to hold on to.
Something to take back with you.
But what if the only real answer
is to leave with empty hands?

The student bowed and said,
"Thank you, Master."

The Master walked away.

Who was thanking whom?
Who was there to bow?

What if all this was just a play?
The **seeking**,
the **questioning**,
the **master**,
the **disciple**.

What if it was all just
a movement of the mind,
chasing its own shadow?

THE LAST ILLUSION.

If you have
understood nothing,
you are *free*.

If you have
understood something,
you are still **trapped**.

You are waiting
for something profound
to happen right now.

Some final twist.

Some deeper meaning behind these words.

But there is none.

You expected the book
to end with some great teaching.

A final, explosive realization
that would shatter everything.

But here you are.
And nothing has happened.

Drop **everything**—
every idea,
every effort,
every understanding.

And if you cannot drop them,
let them burn by themselves.

Now,
what remains?

Not a question.
Not an answer.

Just **this**.

Burn This Book

If you have
reached the end
and feel enlightened,
throw this book away.

If you have
reached the end
and feel confused,
read it again.

If you have
reached the end
and feel nothing—
you are free.

You have spent your life
searching,
collecting,
assembling
pieces of wisdom
like a shrine to some
final answer.

But what if there is no answer?
What if the search itself is the illusion?

You wanted truth.

You wanted liberation.

You wanted something to hold on to,
something to take back with you.

But the moment you hold on,
you are lost again.

Let go of everything,
even this.

NO BOOK CAN SAVE YOU.

Books are cages,
even this one.

Words are traps,
even these.

Every time you name something,
you separate yourself from it.
Every time you define truth,
you turn it into a lie.

This book was never meant to
give you anything.
It was meant to take everything away.

If you carry it like a treasure,
you have missed the point.
If you turn it into a teaching,
you have built another prison.

Truth is not in words.
It is not in pages.
It is not something that
can be passed from one hand
to another.

*A monk carried scriptures
wherever he went, believing they held
the key to freedom.
One day, the wind blew them
into the fire.*

He laughed and walked on.

LET IT ALL BURN.

There is nothing to understand anymore.
Nothing to practice.
Nothing to seek.

Burn this book.

Burn your beliefs.

Burn your search.

And if you cannot burn them,
let them rot.
Let them fall away like
dead leaves in the wind.

You do not need another teaching.
You do not need another master.
You do not need another path.

The **problem** is not with the path.
The **problem** is not with the technique.
The **problem** is not with the teachings.

It is **you**.

The moment you find a path,
the **ego** makes it an identity.
The moment you learn a technique,
the **ego** takes pride in practicing it.
The moment you hear the truth,
the **ego** wears it like a badge.

The ego does not fight against
the spiritual path—it consumes it.
It turns meditation
into an achievement,
enlightenment into a title,
wisdom into another thing
to possess.

And so,
what could have been a fire
that burns the self to ash
becomes just another ornament
on the self's altar.

You have spent your life
peeling layers,
breaking illusions,
tearing down walls—
only to find that
what you were searching for
was never hidden.

It was here
before the questions.
Before the answers.
Before the seeker.

If there is still something left to hold,
you are still carrying a weight.
If there is still something left to understand,
you are still lost in the mind.

And when there is nothing left—

No self,
no search,
no seeker—

See what remains.